Original title:
The Poetry of Parallel Universes

Copyright © 2025 Creative Arts Management OÜ
All rights reserved.

Author: Ronan Whitfield
ISBN HARDBACK: 978-1-80567-834-2
ISBN PAPERBACK: 978-1-80567-955-4

Altars of Alternate Time

In a world where toast lands buttered,
Cats sing ballads, completely unuttered.
Bicycles ride themselves with glee,
While squirrels plan their grand jubilee.

Coffee brews itself with a grin,
And fish play chess, who knows who'll win?
Worms wear suits and charm delight,
In gardens where moonbeams spark excitement.

Constellations of What Might Be

Stars in pajamas twinkle at night,
As giggling comets take their flight.
Jupiter dances the hula with glee,
While Mars debates if it's really a pea.

Asteroids hosting street fairs so bright,
With candy floss clouds that fill the night.
Pluto builds snowmen, freezing his feet,
In a solar system, where life's a treat.

Cities Unseen

There's a city where candy grows on trees,
And everyone's allergic to sneezes.
Broccoli wears a fancy tux,
With kale as a sidekick, full of plucks.

Skyscrapers made of bubblegum,
Where zebras play drums, creating a hum.
The mayor is a wise, old iguana,
His speeches always cause a persona.

Resonance of Divergent Paths

Paths that twist like a pretzel's cheer,
Lead to destinations both far and near.
Where cheeseburgers float and pastries swim,
And penguins teach dance to the whim.

At crossroads where laughter truly bends,
And clocks tick backwards, making amends.
Each choice a jester, pulling a prank,
In life's great circus, we all must thank.

Mysteries of the Multiverse

In one world, cats wear hats,
Sipping tea and chatting gats.
In another, fish climb trees,
Nibbling on a soft cheese.

A world where cows play chess,
Debating who's the best in dress.
And in a realm of dancing mice,
They twirl in shoes, oh so nice!

Verses in the Void

In a galaxy made of cheese,
Aliens dance in the breeze.
They throw moon pies at passing stars,
While sipping light from Mars!

One universe with flying pigs,
Doing the cha-cha in fancy rigs.
They laugh and spin in the milky way,
Saying, 'Why not? It's Tuesday!'

Tides of Possibility

A world where socks have minds of their own,
Taking trips while their owners moan.
They plan a heist at midnight's bell,
To steal a cookie, oh what the smell!

In another, frogs wear tiny cloaks,
Schmoozing with the world's best folks.
They croak out jokes that make you laugh,
And take their bread with a dash of chaff.

Realms of Untold Stories

In a land where toast can converse,
Popping up with rhymes quite terse.
They argue crumbs of breakfast fate,
While jellybeans cultivate debate!

A universe where clocks run slow,
Tick-tocking to a silly show.
They plan pranks on all who dare,
To steal their time, it's only fair!

Songs of the Untraveled Road

In a world where cats can drive,
They cruise in style, oh what a jive!
With leather jackets, shades on tight,
They rule the streets by day and night.

The roads are paved with cheese and fun,
And every stop has ice cream, yum!
Bicycles sprout wings to soar,
While squirrels plot to start a war.

A toaster sings a pop-filled tune,
While dancing dishes shake the moon.
In a universe not far away,
Bananas decide when to break ballet.

But when the sun begins to set,
The traffic light turns into a pet.
It wags its tail, puts on a show,
As giggles ripple, high and low.

Fragments of the Real and Unreal

In a place where shadows paint the ground,
Llamas wear hats and prance around.
Pancakes grow on trees, oh so sweet,
Bouncing jellybeans dance on their feet.

Tea parties held by frogs in ties,
Debating boldly, oh so wise!
They spill the tea on cosmic trends,
While ants unravel how time bends.

Now giraffes juggle with ease and flair,
As puddles giggle, bodies in the air.
Every drop can tell a tale,
Of dragons learning to ride a snail.

The sky's a canvas, painted bright,
With crayons tickling stars at night.
In every corner, life unfurls,
Oh, the joy of both our worlds!

Novels of Another Kind

Once upon a time in candyland,
Chocolate rivers, oh so grand.
A fish in boots wrote tales of cheer,
While marshmallow bunnies played the sphere.

Bookshelves dance and sing out loud,
As storylines form a wiggly crowd.
Where socks can talk and giggle too,
And every sentence starts with 'moo.'

Plot twists served with sprinkles on top,
Characters bubble and twist, they hop.
A ghost who's afraid of his own fuss,
Cries too loud but never makes a fuss.

In spaceships made of sugar and cream,
Dreamers whisper chocolatey dreams.
With laughter echoing through each page,
In a world where whimsy takes the stage.

Horizons Unbounded

In skies of purple and green delight,
Unicorns high-five clouds in flight.
Rainbows wear socks with stripes galore,
While old winds help the seaweed score.

Bubbles bounce, filled with giggle gas,
As time flows softly, like bladder grass.
They wrap around the duck with glee,
As he quacks out the next mystery.

Fish sing karaoke, quite confused,
Telling tales of dreams poorly used.
While rubber ducks hold dinner dates,
Discussing which way the world rotates.

Oh, to live in a world sublime,
Where every moment feels like rhyme.
With laughter echoing strong and clear,
Horizons stretch, oh my dear!

Echoes of the Infinite

In one world, cats wear hats,
And dogs debate in purple spats.
Fish ride bikes, making waves,
While toast and jam play hide-and-seek braves.

In another, clocks tick backward,
And squirrels sing like loud rock-bards.
Pies float gently in the air,
As jellybeans sprout sweet green hair.

Round and round, the worlds spin fast,
Where every oddity's a blast.
Fish have dreams of flying high,
While clouds throw pies that make us sigh.

Glimmers of Other Realms

In one realm, naps are a sport,
Where snoring is the main report.
Elephants dance in tutus grand,
And bumblebees teach Frisbee on sand.

Rainbows pour from coffee cups,
While cupcakes dance with silly pups.
Glitter rains on Wednesday nights,
And unicorns host karaoke fights.

With laughter ringing through the sky,
A jester's joke will always fly.
Every giggle breaks the ground,
In endless fun where joy is found.

Constellations in Collision

Stars play tag in cosmic weather,
While black holes trip on tethered tether.
Galaxies wear their socks askew,
And meteors dance in a polka crew.

In an odd corner of the night,
Comets juggle in sheer delight.
Planets swap their favorite hats,
While aliens toast with squishy vats.

Here, moonbeams slide on banana peels,
And laughter turns to tasty meals.
Every collision brings a cheer,
As gravity tickles all too near.

Verses on the Edge of Reality

Beyond the edge, where jests unfold,
A world of giggles waits, so bold.
Penguins salsa in tuxedo flair,
While rain showers sprinkle candy rare.

Butterflies write their own tales,
Riding bicycles with fluffy tails.
Mice in suits hold grand debates,
While hungry wolves swap fun for plates.

Here, logic takes a silly leave,
And every thought would make you grieve.
Yet on this edge, we dance and spin,
With laughter shared, it's bliss we win.

Whispers Beyond Dimensions

In a world where cats can sing,
And toast pops up with wings.
The trees wear hats and dance around,
As laughter echoes, joy abound.

A squirrel drives a tiny car,
Chasing nuts that shine like stars.
With pancakes flipping through the air,
Their syrup smiles, a sweet affair.

A fish in boots does square the dance,
With flying pigs that take a chance.
Umbrellas bloom on sunny days,
In this wacky, endless maze.

So let us twirl through winding lanes,
Where every thought's a bit insane.
In whispers soft across the night,
We find the strange, delightful light.

Verses of Alternate Worlds

A universe where dogs can talk,
They gossip while we take a walk.
Turtles run and rabbits fly,
As marshmallows bump along the sky.

In one strange realm, the clocks are shaped
Like crazy hats that friends once draped.
Tea is brewed in a wild shoe,
Sipping laughter 'til our cheeks turn blue.

Dreams take flight on bicycles,
Riding past the bubble pools.
Goldfish hosts a grand ballet,
As flamingos lead the grand café.

So let us stroll through every door,
Each step reveals a little more.
In every twist, a giggle lingers,
With silly fun, we dance on fingers.

Dreams in Shattered Mirrors

In a room where mirrors smile back,
Reflecting jokes along the track.
A world where socks can wear a tie,
With noses waggling to the sky.

The clocks are soft and tickle too,
As jellybeans come into view.
A riddle lives on every wall,
With orange cats that gently sprawl.

A dance of chairs on busy nights,
They whirl about in neon lights.
With lollipops that glow and gleam,
We float along in silly dream.

In shards of glass, we see the fun,
Where skates on spoons outshine the sun.
With laughter bouncing, pure delight,
We skip through shadows, full of light.

A Dance of Divergent Paths

Two paths diverge in bubble gum,
One sings sweetly, one is dumb.
Pigs in tutus jump and twirl,
While clever frogs spin in a whirl.

In every twist, a pizza flies,
With pepperoni-winking eyes.
Balloons that giggle kiss the ground,
As unicorns prance all around.

A drink of lemonade that pops,
Sprinkling joy with quirky hops.
Confetti clouds and sunny snails,
Are chasing tales on glitter trails.

So take my hand, let's skip and sway,
In worlds where laughter rules the day.
With silly charms and joyful paths,
We dance through life, escaping math.

Veils of Forgotten Paths

In one world, I'm a cat,
Chasing shadows and cheese.
In another, I'm a brat,
Riding bikes with such ease.

My fish thinks he's a bird,
He flaps his fins in vain.
In dreams, he's never heard,
Of gravity's silly chain.

One coffee shop, two worlds,
One barista, two cups.
I spill the milk, it swirls,
Creating other hiccups.

Lost socks make a rebellion,
In galaxies unknown.
They dance without a felon,
Making mischief alone.

Dimensions of Emerging Light

In one lane, I wear a crown,
Made of spaghetti and sauce.
In the next, I'm a clown,
Driving a tiny pink horse.

My toaster sings a tune,
In symphony with my jam.
In the evening, under moon,
It plays footsie with the ham.

There's a universe of frogs,
Wearing boots and giving tea.
In the rain, they write blogs,
About hops and jubilee.

With each flip of a page,
You find yet another shock.
In my life's circus stage,
I'm also a talking clock.

Mosaics of Concurrent Lives

In one life, I'm a wizard,
With magic wands and spells.
In another, I'm a lizard,
Who juggles tiny bells.

My dreams play hopscotch bold,
On my bed made of light.
They jump and bounce, uncontrolled,
Turning dark into bright.

In a corner, there's a goat,
Wearing glasses, quite refined.
He's lost the will to gloat,
Reading novels, unconfined.

There's a salad in a hat,
Whispering secrets of greens.
In a world spin like that,
Who needs the average means?

Alternates in Verse

In a universe rotated,
I'm a sandwich with a tune.
Each bite is celebrated,
As I glide past the moon.

Meanwhile, my socks engage,
In a dance-off with my shoes.
They twirl across the stage,
Defying all the rules.

Aliens sip my tea,
Complaining it's too hot.
They burst out laughing, see,
As the kettle starts to trot.

I flip through stories wide,
And find the absurd true.
In each twist and each stride,
I'm made of all I knew.

Distorted Reflections

In a world where cats can cook,
With hats that dance and fish that look.
A toaster sings a morning tune,
While spoons play jazz beneath the moon.

A clock that runs on jelly beans,
Plays hide and seek in silly scenes.
The chairs all gossip, quite the fuss,
As purple llamas ride the bus.

A penguin juggles in the park,
While elephants get ready to spark.
With ice cream trees and soda springs,
This twisted realm just laughs and sings.

But if you blink, it all can change,
To normal far, but still quite strange.
In every turn, a giggle's found,
In this mad world of fun abound.

Ballad of the Forgotten Realms

In a realm where socks can talk,
And sticky notes form a block.
The knights don't ride, they roller skate,
While dragons play at checkmate fate.

A wizard tripped on shoelace strings,
And stumbled into clownish things.
His spells confused, they turned to cake,
And laughter followed every quake.

The trolls are chefs, they bake with love,
While unicorns soar high above.
A dance-off sparks a fierce delight,
In battles fought with silly sights.

Yet in this place where chuckles reign,
Not once a hero feels the pain.
For every quest, a bubble burst,
And joys combine, for laughs they thirst.

Maps of Imaginary Places

In lands where jellyfish wear shoes,
And blueberry trees refuse to snooze.
A river flows with chocolate sauce,
And cozy bears play hopscotch across.

The mountains hum a tuneful song,
As flamingos strut and dance along.
With maps that twist and turn on cue,
To find a treasure made of goo.

A pirate ship that sails on air,
With crew of squirrels beyond compare.
They search for gold in marshmallow caves,
In these wild lands, it misbehaves.

And if you wander, stop and stare,
You'll find a rhino with bright hair.
With laughter echoing everywhere,
These maps of joy lead without a care.

Currents of the Unexplored

In currents where the fish wear ties,
And sailboats giggle with surprise.
The waves with bubble gum do clash,
As sea turtles make a daring splash.

A captain with a silly hat,
Commands a crew of curious cats.
They wander off on quests so grand,
To find the kingdom made of sand.

With treasure chests that hold balloons,
And mermaids strumming silly tunes.
The ocean floor, a vibrant stage,
Where every creature earns a wage.

So dive beneath and join the fun,
In worlds where every day's a pun.
For in these depths, one can't ignore,
The laughter flowing evermore.

Shadows of the Unseen

In a world where socks go missing,
Chasing them like little dreams,
Finding them in odd dimensions,
Teasing portals with silly schemes.

A cat speaks in riddles, a fish walks,
Every joke a cosmic punchline,
Universes are just like our talks,
Where humor bends time, oh so fine!

Here, pancakes dance to a joyful beat,
And toast jumps up, calling us sweet,
Gravity plays tricks on the unawares,
Floaty laughs as reality flares!

As I trip on a quark in my shoe,
I wink to my twin in a tutu,
Life is a series of wacky spins,
In shadows where silliness begins.

Fragments of Existence

In a universe where ducks wear hats,
And time ticks sideways like a cat,
I sip my tea from a shoe today,
Wondering what the spoons would say.

Here, rain falls up and clouds are green,
The grass does flips, what a scene!
My thoughts collide in a cosmic race,
Chasing giggles through time and space.

Pigeons negotiate with squirrels for bread,
While bouncing stars dance overhead,
Each moment's a playful little tease,
Bending reality like a merry breeze!

Fragments are laughs in this woven world,
Where time loops back and joy is swirled,
Frogs wear capelets, and rabbits chase,
In a fantastical, funny embrace.

Routes to the Unreached

Maps scribbled in silly delight,
Guide us to streets of day and night,
Where marshmallow clouds flit and sway,
Always leading us astray!

A bus made of jelly wobbles by,
With passengers laughing, oh my!
Each stop is a giggle, a playful pun,
On this ride, we twist and run.

Roads split like jokes in a comedy show,
Where even the winds play tag, you know?
We skip through colors, hop through frames,
Each turn revealing hilarious games!

A highway made of spaghetti lies,
Underneath a ketchup sky,
We twirl toward the unreached by chance,
On noodles of laughter, we dance.

Surges Across the Unknown

In the depths of apple pies that fly,
Giggling at numbers as they sigh,
An old toaster serves wisdom, you see,
While bananas plot to join the spree.

In a surge of giggles, my socks reveal,
They're staging a show with a grand appeal,
Outside my window, worlds collide,
Parades of fun, an absurd ride.

Waves of silliness crash on shore,
As jellybeans chant and rattle, oh, what a score!
Each bubble bursts with uncharted glee,
Frolicking through joys, wild and free!

Across the unknown, we bounce and sway,
Chasing quirks on a zany holiday,
Surges of laughter echo the night,
In strange realms, everything feels just right.

Rhythms of the Unseen

In a realm where socks can dance,
Peanut butter plays in France,
Jellybeans rain from the sky,
And cat wizards learn to fly.

Time ticks backward, laughs a lot,
Trees wear sneakers, what a thought!
Turtles croon in harmony,
While fish do stand-up comedy.

Bananas walk with wobbly grace,
In a world that's a wacky place,
Cars cartwheel down the avenue,
As penguins swap their suits for blue.

So flip your mind to foolish ways,
Where whimsy reigns and humor plays,
What if the world was upside down?
We'd wear a giggle like a crown!

Shadows of What Could Be

In the shadows, ducks recite,
Silly poems every night,
Bubblegum trees sway in rhyme,
Tickled stars dance out of time.

A toaster dreams of flying high,
With all the crumbs that say goodbye,
Toaster strudels float like kites,
While shoes play tag with the street lights.

In this realm of giggly schemes,
Where every clock has silly dreams,
Rain has a flavor—candy sweet,
And shoes do cha-cha on their feet.

Children throw sprinkles in the air,
Unicorns chat without a care,
We laugh aloud, then sneeze confetti,
In a world that's far too petty!

Liminal Landscapes

Step through doors of silly sights,
Where jellybeans hold rocket fights,
Kangaroos on roller skates,
Compete with dancing dinner plates.

Clouds of popcorn drift and swirl,
As cupcakes twirl with every whirl,
Each blade of grass sings a mocking tune,
With dancing spoons beneath the moon.

A world of dreams, bizarre yet bright,
Where spaghetti takes a playful flight,
To meet the forks who serve the pie,
While happy pies all sing goodbye.

We skip through colors, laugh and twirl,
In this whimsical, dazzling world,
So take a leap and dare to be,
In the land of pure hilarity!

Poetic Constellations

Stars wear hats and float like dreams,
While comets burst with silly beams,
Galaxies all hold a parade,
Of fuzzy aliens unafraid.

In this sky of doodles bright,
Asteroids juggle all night,
One twirls, and then another flips,
As planets laugh and do their skits.

A black hole hums a jaunty tune,
As spaceships line up for the noon,
Martians share their quirky talk,
While meteors do a moonwalk.

Here in this cosmic jest so grand,
Invisible creatures share a band,
So hold on tight and soak it in,
For giggles are the paths we spin!

Starlit Reflections

In a world where cats wear hats,
And dogs can dance with glee,
I sip my tea with a talking bee,
As disco stars wink at me.

Twinkling lights on the ceiling,
Hopping between earth and Mars,
I try to teach my couch to sing,
While my goldfish plays on guitars.

One day I'll catch a comet's tail,
And ride it through the sky,
To tickle drunk meteors,
While I ask the moon to fly.

Curious dreams, they bounce and prance,
In these oddball realms we roam,
Each giggle spills a rainbow trail,
With stars that feel like home.

Threads of Cosmic Tapestries

In a universe made of spaghetti,
Where noodles twist and tangle,
I trip on garlic knots, oh how petty,
And tango with a dapper angle.

The stars are chefs, they sizzle bright,
With pancakes flying high,
Jellybeans rain in the pale moonlight,
While martian squirrels pass by.

I found a sock on Jupiter's shore,
Its mate's lost in the void,
As I knit a scarf for a grumpy dinosaur,
Who declares himself overjoyed.

With stitches made of stardust dreams,
I craft a cloak of fun,
Every thread weaves a joke, it seems,
In this cosmos, we all run.

Parallel Echoes

In a world where laughter makes a sound,
That only ducks can hear,
I moonwalk on marshmallow ground,
And toast to every cheer.

Where shadows tell joke after joke,
And laugh until they snore,
I've befriended a silly spokes-doke,
Who claims he fought a dinosaur.

The mirrors crack, and giggles dance,
With echoes chasing dreams,
I skip through laughs and silly prance,
Rotating in cosmic beams.

Every bubble burst brings a laugh,
In shapes that twist and play,
For every joke is a photograph,
Of ridiculousness on display.

Horizons of Possibility

On a raccoon's rocket ship I ride,
To planets made of cream,
Where every gopher knows how to glide,
And fluff the clouds with dreams.

Dancing on rainbows, we zip and zoom,
With unicorns cracking jokes,
Each giggle fuels this cosmic broom,
As we zoom past silly folks.

To a realm where pineapples wear shades,
And sing with glee at noon,
I'll twirl with trees in their leafy parades,
While jiggle bugs play the tune.

With horizons stretched beyond the mind,
Adventures propped on humor,
As the stars align, all kind,
In a universe that's a rumor.

Orbits of the Demonstrably Impossible

In a world where cows can fly,
They serenade the passing pie.
Cats wear hats and dance a jig,
While frogs debate the cosmic fig.

Socks exchange their secret schemes,
As toasters toast their pointed dreams.
The sky is green, the grass is blue,
Who knew the sun could be such a boo?

Ducks perform their morning cheer,
While jellybeans dance on the beer.
Every streetlamp tells a joke,
To the playful clouds that float and poke.

In this realm of silly cheer,
Bacon floats, and cheese can steer.
Life's a game where nothing's real,
But who can doubt a dancing meal?

Threads of Cosmic Convergence

In a universe of tangled yarn,
The spaghetti makes a fine alarm.
Pasta planets whirl and spin,
While meatballs invade the nearest fin.

Aliens sport a chicken suit,
Debating if it's time to loot.
Galaxy elders knit their socks,
In a fabric full of paradox.

The stars will tease in every blink,
As donuts plot on how to think.
With sprinkles raining from above,
They sprinkle space with lots of love.

Cosmic threads, so bright and soft,
In this chaos, we drift aloft.
We laugh at everything we see,
Amidst the strands of cosmic glee!

Interwoven Chronicles

Once a fish decided to roam,
Its gills penned pages of foam.
Each wave a word, so full of flair,
As bubbles shared the latest dare.

Worms wear bowties, quite absurd,
While daisies shout the latest word.
Grasshoppers hold a talent show,
And win with leaps that steal the glow.

Starlight plays a symphony grand,
When spoons and forks start a band.
They ukulele in a moony bar,
While veggies cheer from a nearby jar.

Thus, the tales find their way,
In every laugh, in every sway.
In worlds where oddness reigns supreme,
We stitch the fabric of the dream.

Tesseracts of Thought

In boxes wrapped around the sun,
Thoughts play tag, oh what fun!
Idea cats chase notion mice,
While synapses roll the dice.

Time jumps in a silly dance,
Wearing mismatched socks by chance.
Every tick and every tock,
A game of hopscotch on a clock.

Brainstorms brew cups of tea,
Inviting cats to share a spree.
Chickens argue with a chair,
About the color of the air.

In dimensions warped and wide,
Thoughts collide and sides collide.
With laughter echoing through the spheres,
The impossible brings jubilant cheers!

Echoed Emotions Across Time

In a world where socks refuse to match,
A cat in boots quips, 'What a catch!'
Mirrors talk back, with cheeky grins,
While spoons claim victory on forks' thin sins.

Time travels in circles, like a roller skate,
Chasing tail while munching on a plate.
Whispers of past lives echo and bounce,
As hiccuped laughter dares to pounce.

Jellybeans rain down from the sky,
As unicorns waltz with a knowing sigh.
Time bumbles and tumbles like a clumsy clown,
In this universe, a frown turns upside down.

Dancing with gravity, it slips and it flops,
While cheese on toast takes awkward hops.
Maybe I'll visit that world made of cheese,
Where pizza is king and veggies just tease.

Labyrinths of Liminality

In hallways lined with spaghetti strands,
Ninjas juggle pickles with sleepy hands.
Doors creak open to odd sounds aglow,
While goldfish debate who can steal the show.

A staircase curls like a questioning vine,
As robots sip tea and consider some wine.
Whimsical whispers tickle the air,
In a realm where cats have their own haircare.

Time takes a step but sidesteps in glee,
As chocolate rain drips from a grand old tree.
Knights made of jelly stumble and sway,
While creatures of fluff come out to play.

Here, gravity giggles and bends to the side,
While turtles in tutus suddenly glide.
Would you take a look at all this delight?
When laughter turns mundane into sheer delight!

Reflections Across the Veil

The mirror's a gossip with secrets to share,
It rolls its eyes as if it can care.
Reflecting on life with a snicker or two,
As peanut butter wishes for jelly to chew.

Flipping pancakes that giggle and scream,
Sometimes reality feels like a dream.
Lions in pajamas hold tea parties bright,
While cacti recite poems every night.

Clouds parade in tutus, a sight to behold,
Whispering tales of brave knights, oh so bold.
Adventures unfurl in laughter and cheer,
In this place where odd just feels so near.

Popcorn kernels burst just to join in the jest,
With each added splash, it's a flavorful quest.
Creativity swirls, an elaborate dance,
In realms of reflection, a comical chance.

Fragments of Different Dreams

In one world, cats wear hats,
And dogs all sing opera in spats.
Meanwhile in a realm quite absurd,
Fish ride bicycles, oh how they've stirred!

A farmer harvests cupcakes galore,
While robots dance on the kitchen floor.
And over the hills, unicorns play,
Baking muffins at the end of the day!

In a land where socks are seen as kings,
They argue about all sorts of things.
Toasters toast bread that sings 'Oh My!'
As waffles do the moonwalk nearby.

So let's gather these tales from afar,
Of worlds where the bizarre is the star.
With laughter and whimsy, we'll explore,
Fragments of dreams that we all adore.

Multiverse Musings

What if penguins ruled the street?
In pinstripe suits, they'd be quite neat.
They'd dance at night, throw fancy galas,
While polar bears sip on sweet piña coladas!

In another world, it's all upside down,
Where jellybeans wear a crown!
Giraffes play chess, with queens so bright,
And life is a cake fight every night!

Imagine a town where everyone's mute,
They communicate through the sound of a flute.
The bicycles glide on rivers of cream,
While everyone lives in a candy dream.

Oh, the musings of worlds yet to see,
Filled with giggles, oh what glee!
Let's jump through the portal, take a chance,
In these universe quirks, let's laugh and dance!

Surreal Serenades

A chicken in shoes, oh what a sight,
Singing tunes on a Saturday night.
With a disco ball shining overhead,
Bouncing to rhythms, enough said!

In a realm where trees sprout lollipops,
And candy clouds rain down on the hops.
Squirrels wear capes as they take flight,
Saving snacks in a comical plight!

Oceans of lemonade, beaches of cake,
While rubber ducks in a parade partake.
Donuts float by on fluffy marshmallows,
In this world ruled by whimsical fellows.

So join the serenade, let's take a bow,
In lands where the strange is the norm somehow.
We'll dance with delight, all worries now wet,
Lost in the laughter, no need to fret!

Convergences of Fate

In one universe, toast knows it's divine,
While pancake cows hold a judgmental line.
They debate over which breakfast is best,
As bacon flies by in a buttery quest!

Bubblegum rain pours from cotton skies,
While cartoon mushrooms wear slapstick ties.
In this dimension where silliness reigns,
Laughter erupts and nothing remains!

Picture this, a land of dancing spoons,
Where forks play jazz under the light of the moons.
Spatulas spin in a frenzied delight,
As vegetables waltz into the night!

So come along, let's carefully weave,
Across these paths where mirth won't leave.
In convergences bright, together we'll find,
The giggles and joy that life's intertwined!

Ungraspable Destinies

In one world, cats play chess,
While dogs are chefs, no less.
In another, fish can fly,
And cows just sit and sigh.

A universe where socks can dance,
While shoes are caught in a romance.
In one, bananas sing out loud,
While oranges draw quite the crowd.

In a realm with jellybean rain,
Spiders juggling, what a gain!
Meanwhile, frogs in tuxedos swim,
At a gala for the whimsy grim.

Each tale, a twist or two,
In lands where nothing's true.
So laugh, my friend, don't be shy,
In this circus of the sky!

Eclipsing Narratives

In one tale, cows surf the waves,
And chickens act like braves.
While in the next, spoons have fights,
And forks hold dramatic nights.

Cats wearing hats read the news,
And rabbits write quirky reviews.
In a different spin, hats can dance,
While shoes have their own romance.

While aliens trade silly jokes,
Mermaids laugh at their weird strokes.
Parallel worlds where the odd is norm,
And breakfast cereals have their own charm.

With surprises you can't foresee,
Every path is filled with glee.
So grab a snack, let's have some fun,
In these realms that leap and run!

Lost in Translation

In one world, trees speak of cheese,
While clouds just float with greatest ease.
In another, toast has sharp wit,
And jam throws shade, it can't quit.

A universe where laughter rains,
And pigeons board the trains.
While cats compose opera songs,
And dogs join in—what could go wrong?

In a reality where tigers knit,
While squirrels hold a comedy bit.
Rabbits in cardigans sip their tea,
Discussing how funny it could be.

So smile, dear friend, it's a treat,
When worlds collide in mirthful beat.
Let laughter lead the way today,
Through translations that twist and play!

Imagined Intersections

In a land where marshmallows fly,
And everyone wears a pie,
Potatoes with sunglasses roam,
Making every day feel like home.

Here, penguins take a train to work,
While mermaids smirk and lurk.
Cacti wearing cowboy hats,
Chat with yo-yos and dancing rats.

Meanwhile, robots paint the sky,
While giraffes try to give a hi.
Inverting norms with joy, it's true,
A fest of quirks for me and you.

So let's skip down this pathless road,
Where wild ideas are freely strode.
With laughter echoing near and far,
In these intersections, we are the stars!

Intersections of Fate and Fantasy

In a realm where socks pair jump,
One finds a shoe atop a stump.
Cats in hats debate their fate,
While wise old frogs just spectate.

Pancakes rain from skies of blue,
With syrup rivers that flow true.
Dancing penguins sing a song,
In this world, you can't go wrong.

Unicorns sip tea on chairs,
While a dragon juggles apples, unaware.
When time is silly, who could care?
In such places, laughter's rare.

Each corner holds a twist of chance,
Where oddments lead us to a dance.
With fate and fancy side by side,
In this wild ride, we take our stride.

Liminal Spaces Between Here and There

In the hallway that bends and sways,
Time does cartwheels, lost in a haze.
Pigeons in bow ties really strut,
While clocks just giggle, what a putt!

A mailbox opens to a dream,
Where every letter's just a meme.
Ovens bake thoughts in golden light,
And shadows play hide-and-seek at night.

Under the rug, a portal waits,
Where lost socks chat on dinner plates.
Here and there, it's hard to know,
If it's a show or all for show.

In these spaces, giggles reign,
Reality bends, we're all insane.
Jump through the door or take the stair,
You'll find a smile waiting there.

Time's Many Faces

A clock with legs runs very fast,
But trips on moments and falls at last.
Seconds wear hats, and minutes can dance,
While hours forget to take a chance.

In a maze of tick-tock surprises,
Each turn reveals quirky disguises.
Time as a jester throws out a pun,
As days cheer on the setting sun.

Wormholes spiral with giggly tunes,
As seconds play chess with old raccoons.
Each tick brings a chuckle, a sigh,
Seconds flail, but never ask why.

In this circus where time plays the fool,
Life's a game with no set rule.
We laugh as we foxtrot through space,
Embracing every silly face.

Colors of Unimaginable Skies

Sky painted in shades of pizza cheese,
With clouds of popcorn that float with ease.
Rainbow squirrels leap with glee,
While sunflowers sing in harmony.

Velvet greens and electric blues,
Just wait for fuchsia to sprout its views.
Lemonade rivers twist and twirl,
As jellybean whales perform a whirl.

Cactus trees boast their fruity hats,
With squirrels harmonizing with the bats.
In this land of peculiar hue,
The skies paint pranks for me and you.

When colors clash and joy collides,
Imagination is what abides.
In vibrant realms where laughter flies,
The world lives bright, no need for lies.

Chasing the Unwritten

In a world where socks have wings,

and bananas turn into kings.

I scribble tales with jellybeans,

while reality giggles at my scenes.

A turtle dances with a fish,

they plot to grant my every wish.

I paint the moon with shades of green,

as mimes perform on an unseen screen.

Forget the rules, let's take a ride,

on a rollercoaster made of pride.

Each twist and turn a quirky joke,

as laughter bubbles in clouds of smoke.

So grab your pen, let's start the chase,

into the lands of absurd space.

With each word spun, let nonsense reign,

in this merry world, we'll break the chain.

Dimensions of Heart and Soul

In a realm where hearts wear hats,
and cats recite in top hats, chitchats.
We skip on clouds of cotton candy,
where all things silly are quite dandy.

A giraffe plays chess with a mouse,
while a frog jumps high in a tiny house.
Love's a dance with mismatched socks,
as we jive past the dawn's gentle knocks.

Ice cream flows like rivers wide,
where every choice is a funny ride.
Jokes bounce around like animated flies,
in a dimension where laughter never dies.

So let's embrace this silly fate,
with love that can make a toaster skate.
For in these depths of the heart's delight,
we'll find the joy that sparks the night.

Gardens of the Mind's Eye

In gardens where umbrellas grow,
and daisies dance like stars in tow.
Each flower whispers a cheeky tune,
that makes the sun wink at the moon.

A hedgehog wears a vibrant coat,
as ladybugs begin to float.
In this paradise of whimsy's call,
laughter blooms and never falls.

Bunnies juggling berries and cheese,
while the breeze carries their giggling tease.
Picnics under apple tree skies,
where ants deliver surprises in pies.

These visions twirl like autumn leaves,
in a world where nonsense weaves.
So let's plant seeds of silly dreams,
and harvest smiles in joyful beams.

Murmurs from Across the Rift

From the rift where shadows play,

come whispers of a bizarre ballet.

Chickens tap dance on purple ground,

as silly secrets spin around.

Marshmallows sail on soda seas,

while we share giggles with buzzing bees.

A comet wears a rubber duck,

as time itself runs out of luck.

In this realm where oddities connect,

every twist elicits pure respect.

Fish fly by on invisible wings,

conjuring laughter through cosmic flings.

So call your friends to join the jest,

in murmurs that put sanity to rest.

Across the rift, we play and thrive,

finding joy in the dive to the archives.

Fabric of Alternate Lives

In one world, cats wear hats,
And dogs recite their chats.
Fish play chess in clear blue skies,
While ants dance in neat ties.

In another realm, spoons can sing,
Bicycles have a fancy bling.
Rain falls up, and so do we,
No more stairs, just a slide to be.

In universes where socks are free,
They rebel, just wait and see.
Chickens fly with wings so grand,
While cows create rock bands.

In a laugh, the worlds collide,
Comedy's the perfect guide.
Each life a joke, a quirky twist,
In every realm, a funny gist.

Harmonies from Beyond

Bananas play the saxophone,
While oranges sing quite alone.
Lettuce leads the funky beat,
And carrots dance with tiny feet.

From worlds where jellybeans do waltz,
Their moves are fluid, never false.
Peas in unison, they cheer,
As cupcakes bring the laughter near.

In tune with time, they skip and slide,
A symphony of silly pride.
Each note a wink, a wink a grin,
In these realms, the fun begins!

From cosmic depths, the humor flows,
With every quirk, it brightly glows.
In every laugh, a spark divine,
As tunes of joy in space align.

Journeys Through the Unwritten

One book whispers tales untold,
Of brave ducks and knights of gold.
In pages where the ink takes flight,
Rabbits duel by afternoon light.

In worlds of prose, a pizza flies,
With toppings that can hypnotize.
Monkeys write the plots for fun,
While squirrels bake muffins in the sun.

Each chapter spins a quirky yarn,
Where flowers play the role of barn.
In stories where the rules are bent,
With every twist, a funny dent.

Adventure calls, with laughter loud,
In every tale, a joyful crowd.
In one swish, the ink does dance,
As lovers waltz in a cheeseball romance.

Celestial Symphonies

Stars wear glasses and read the news,
While comets sport the latest shoes.
Planets play hopscotch in the void,
Creating tunes that can't be floyd.

The moon hums softly, a gentle tease,
As asteroids jiggle in the breeze.
Galaxies twirl, a grand ballet,
In cosmic rhythms, they laugh and sway.

In constellations, cats play chess,
With cosmic fish, they feel no stress.
Every twinkle, a joke to share,
In this humorous, stellar air.

With every burst of solar fun,
The universe shines—each day's a pun.
In the expanse, the laughter flies,
As spirits soar across the skies.

Journeys Through the Unknown

In one world, cats wear hats,
And dance a ballet on the mats.
Dogs serve tea with flying pies,
While cows run races in disguise.

In another, socks make grand plans,
To rule the world with tiny hands.
They wiggle, jiggle, all in glee,
Telling tales of mystery.

Yet in the third, a toaster speaks,
It tells of bread's adventurous peaks.
With buttered dreams and jelly laughs,
They toast to interstellar paths.

Through portals of whimsy, we slide fast,
Chasing shadows of futures past.
In these realms of giggles and cheer,
Every absurdity feels so near.

Eclipses of Distant Dreams

Under a sky with two suns bright,
Kangaroos joust in a playful fight.
They laugh as they bounce on purple beams,
Creating chaos for silly dreams.

In dreams where clouds are candy fluff,
Children ride unicorns, oh so tough!
They eat rainbows and dance on air,
With gummy bears, free from all care.

An octopus wearing roller skates,
Dances with whales in equal fates.
Both sing songs from a pirate ship,
While mermaids join with a glittery flip.

Eclipses bring giggles from far away,
Where every weird thought has its say.
In twinkling stars, we find our place,
With smiles that stretch across space.

Echoes of Infinity

In a world where pajamas reign,
Socks are the rulers, quite insane.
They plot to conquer, oh what a sight,
While the shirts rejoice in their plight.

A fish in a suit with a briefcase too,
Negotiates deals in a coffee brew.
He smiles wide with a wink and a nod,
As seaweed plays the role of a god.

In another lane, bananas talk,
They gossip about the latest sock.
Laughing loud with their fruity peers,
Creating giggles that last for years.

The echoes of laughter bounce back and forth,
In dimensions of dreams that measure their worth.
With jests so busy, they'll never cease,
In spirals of joy, we find our peace.

Fractured Realities

In one place, teapots sprout legs,
And dance on tables with sassy pegs.
They spin and twirl with a chipper cheer,
While spoons cheer on from yonder sphere.

There's a universe where tacos sing,
And chicken wings have their own bling.
They croon about tasty, saucy tales,
While garlic bread woos with buttery scales.

In cosmic realms of silly sights,
Giraffes wear glasses and have tight fights.
Sipping smoothies, they judge the flair,
Of all who wander without a care.

Fractured stories collide, never shy,
In laughter, they connect, like stars in the sky.
Here, absurdity thrives like a flower,
In dimensions where giggles hold all the power.

Echoes in the Infinite

In one realm, cats wear hats,
And dogs have fancy shoes.
The squirrels toast with donuts,
While rabbits bake some brews.

Just down the lane, the fish can fly,
They swim through the tall trees.
The clouds are made of cotton candy,
And unicorns sneeze out bees.

A world where clocks just smile and wink,
Each tick's a silly tune.
As elephants dance the cha-cha,
Underneath a purple moon.

If only we could visit there,
And leave behind our cares.
With laughter echoing all around,
And joy in cosmic layers.

Fractured Realities

In one place, cows are rock stars,
Their moos echo through the bars.
The farmers cheer and dance along,
While pigs play air guitars.

In another, forks converse with spoons,
At quaint little dinner chats.
They gossip about the plates they meet,
And the latest trends in mats.

There's even a land where shadows talk,
And in jokes they love to weave.
They tell of day when night went mad,
And stole the sun to grieve.

What a world of wackiness indeed,
Where nonsense reigns the day!
Full of whimsy and laughter,
In a fractured, funny way.

Whispers Between Worlds

In whispers, worlds collide and spin,
Where fish drive cars and swim.
The trees wear pants and hats askew,
While owls sing jazz on a whim.

Another realm you wouldn't guess,
Where socks refuse to pair.
They dance alone in oddball waltzes,
And giggle without a care.

Meanwhile, the sun tells silly jokes,
And the moon just rolls its eyes.
Starfish laugh at all the fuss,
While planets connive in disguise.

In these whispers of the strange and fun,
Imagination takes flight.
As we skip through bizarre landscapes,
Chasing joy both day and night.

Threads of Alternate Dreams

In a world of dreams, the clouds are cheese,
And the stars are made of sprinkles.
Kangaroos play hopscotch with the moon,
As the sun in laughter crinkles.

A realm of jellybean rivers flows,
With gumdrop bridges wide.
Where elephants wear shiny shoes,
And rainbows are their guide.

One universe holds ticklish trees,
That laugh when you give a hug.
With grass that giggles when you tread,
And flowers that feel snug.

These threads of dreams weave weird and bright,
Creating fun with ease.
In corners of our minds they dance,
Bringing smiles like gentle breeze.

Fluctuating Frequencies

In one realm, cats can talk,
They gossip while we walk,
Dogs wear glasses, think they're cool,
Teaching squirrels to swim in a pool.

In another, pizza flies high,
With pepperoni clouds in the sky,
Everyone dances with a twist,
And devours pies that cannot be missed.

At lunch, they munch on rainbow fries,
While unicorns sing lullabies,
Time's a prankster, darts and dives,
Juggling clocks, it's all alive.

So if you find the world quite odd,
Just blame it on the cosmic rod,
For every shift, a giggle waits,
In strange lands where laughter creates.

Mystical Crossroads

At a junction, frogs wear hats,
Debating about the world's chitchats,
One insists that cows can fly,
While owls sell ice cream, oh my, oh my!

The time travelers race by, oh dear,
In shoes that squeak and disappear,
They trip over donuts, what a show,
While ducks in tutus steal the dough.

Round and round, the signs say "Go!"
But they just spin like a carnival show,
A lion on a skateboard zooms,
While dreaming of intergalactic rooms.

So take a seat on this twirly ride,
With unicorns prancing at your side,
Where whimsies bloom like flowers bright,
And every glance is pure delight.

Patterns in the Cosmos

Stars wear glasses to get a view,
Of cupcakes and jellybeans that grew,
Planets pirouette in silly dance,
Chasing comets with a cheeky glance.

Galaxies shaped like giant pies,
Float through the sky with joyful sighs,
Alien chefs bake from stardust dough,
While asteroids are hidden in the dough.

Silly shadows giggle and sway,
As colors shimmy, bounce, and play,
Dreams come alive with each squiggly line,
Crafting worlds where unicorns shine.

So grab a wink from the evening star,
You might just meet a friendly czar,
In a universe where fun's the rule,
And laughter brings joy, it's so cool!

Reflections of Fanatic Adventures

In a world where socks can sing,
And rubber ducks are the real king,
Hopping bunnies fly to the moon,
While bananas dance to a jazzy tune.

Meanwhile, fish play chess in the sea,
Arguing over who's next to be,
The cat on the shore with a monocle,
Judges each move, oh what a spectacle!

Magical portals in the old fridge door,
Lead to lands where ice cream galore,
Rains on Tuesdays, or so they say,
When sprinkles tumble and kids can play.

So pack your bags, let's travel far,
To places where dreams are bizarre,
With giggles and whispers, we'll explore,
In a universe where fun is the core!

Patterns in the Fabric of Space

In a world where cats can rule,
And dogs are taught to play the fool.
Birds wear hats and dance all night,
While fish in suits take flight with delight.

Time's a rubber band, oh what a mess,
It bounces back with a giggle, no less.
When clocks are silly, they tick-tock and spin,
Reality's fabric wears a broad, goofy grin.

Granny's knitting socks from stars,
While grandpa races past in shiny cars.
Planets trade places in a dizzying whirl,
Could this be the day a tomato might twirl?

Now join the fun, it's never a bore,
With jellybeans bouncing from ceiling to floor.
Universes laugh at their cosmic pranks,
As we dance together in colorful ranks.

Laughter in Another Life

In this realm, cows sing opera loud,
While sheep wear shades and dance in a crowd.
Pigs in pajamas do a cha-cha slide,
Everyone's giggling, enjoying the ride.

Clouds are pillows, rain tastes like cake,
Every mistake's just a bath for a snake.
Socks wear socks, oh what a sight,
While donkeys debate the stars at night.

Gravity's silly, floats up then down,
Laughter's the king, in this topsy town.
Doors open sideways, then close like a grin,
And I've heard that broccoli just learned to spin.

Friends are like stars, shining so bright,
In this other life, they dance with delight.
So hold on tight, enjoy the whirl,
Another life awaits; give it a twirl!

When Stars Align Differently

Stars wear shades of polka dot blue,
And comets play hopscotch, just for a view.
The moon struts about in a feathered dress,
While Mars juggles asteroids, no need to impress.

Each constellation has a sleek dance move,
With galaxy disco, we all find our groove.
Planets pop popcorn and laugh at the fuss,
As oversized ducks approach in a bus.

In this dimension of shimmering cheer,
Black holes decant drinks with a bubbly leer.
Shooting stars tickle our ears as they fly,
Saying, 'Wish upon us!' – oh, what a lie.

So let's tug at the strings of this cosmic play,
Where laughter's the key to keeping gloom at bay.
Stars align to show us the craziest sights,
As we sing to the rhythm of infinite nights.

Lost in the Multiverse's Embrace

In a realm where giggles echo and play,
Cats can do backflips in the strangest way.
Accidents become exciting plans,
As jellybeans waltz with wooden cans.

Every road leads to a funny surprise,
With rivers of chocolate, oh my, how time flies!
Dancing on rainbows, we skip with glee,
On sidewalks of bubblegum, come join me!

Balloons can talk, giving advice on a song,
While trees tell tales of where things went wrong.
Gravity pulls on a mischievous string,
Spellbinding laughter in this magical fling.

So come take a step through this world of fun,
Where hedgehogs wear shoes and turtles can run.
In this embrace, everything's silly and bright,
Together we'll laugh until morning's first light.

Whimsies of Wandering Worlds

In a realm where socks have wings,
And jellybeans are kings,
Cats high-five with glee,
While frogs sip herbal tea.

A duck wears a tux and ties,
As unicorns sell fries,
Mice play chess with cheese,
And everyone shouts, "Cheese!"

Balloon flowers take flight,
Dancing through the night,
Lollipops paint the breeze,
As giggles float with ease.

In this land of pure delight,
Where laughter shines so bright,
The rules bend and break,
Just watch the joy it makes!

Divergence in the Fabric of Time

Clockhands twist and twirl,
As fish wear hair in curls,
Time sometimes takes a nap,
In that cozy, fluffy gap.

Socks may walk without feet,
While pancakes dance to the beat,
Gravity hops around,
In this chaos, joy is found.

Monkeys rhyme upon the moon,
Swinging softly with a tune,
Sandwiches in tuxedos,
Serve tea from their toes.

When history laughs out loud,
While future wears a cloud,
The clocks may tick and tock,
But nothing can stop the shock!

Singularity's Shadow

In shadows where giggles collide,
A penguin takes a slide,
Jellyfish wear tiny hats,
While squirrels chat with bats.

Pizzas fly on wheels,
As ketchup loses its appeals,
Forks and spoons hold a dance,
In a world of pure romance.

What if bugs could run the show,
With disco lights and a glow?
Chickens cluck in harmony,
While toasters sing a glee.

When paradoxes meet at dawn,
And cows all sprout a yawn,
The universe jests with ease,
Tickle the cosmos, if you please!

Lyrics from Lost Futures

Ovens bake with silly tunes,
While robots dance with spoons,
Horses dream of flying high,
Wishing on a pizza pie.

In futures odd, where we trip,
On rainbow roads we slip,
Bananas lead a parade,
As time bends in charade.

Fish in top hats take a stroll,
Underneath the candy bowl,
Magicians pull out rabbits,
That giggle like small habbits.

Oh, leap through dreams anew,
Where every wish comes true,
Sing with worlds unbound,
In laughter, joy is found!

Reflections in the Glass

In a world where cats wear hats,
And dogs can earn their stripes,
Mirrors hold their laughter tight,
And squirrels ride on tricycles, yipes!

Glass houses filled with giggles,
Where goldfish dance a jig,
Pineapples play the trumpet loud,
While onions don a wig!

Reflections of a wobbly fate,
As llamas bend to sing,
With jellybeans for shoes to wear,
They prance and hop in spring!

So peer into that window bright,
You'll find a world askew,
With wacky sights and silly sounds,
Embrace the bizarre view!

Shadows of a Different Dawn

In a place where pancakes fly,
And syrup drips from trees,
Roosters crow in perfect rhyme,
Despite the buzzing bees.

Sunflowers wear sunglasses cool,
And dance to funky beats,
While shadows stretch and twist around,
In rhythm with their feet.

An owl hoots in Morse code talk,
To squirrels on the run,
They plot a heist for golden nuts,
While giggling in the sun!

With laughter echoing at dawn,
What wonders twist and twirl,
In shadows of a different time,
Where whimsy starts to whirl!

Beyond the Veil of Existence

Beneath the veil, the socks have fun,
They play their silly games,
Leading laundry lives of joy,
With mismatched names and claims.

The teacups chatter day and night,
With sugar cubes in tow,
While spoons debate their etiquette,
In a swirling tea-time show!

A garden where the veggies laugh,
As carrots play charades,
Beans recite their poetry,
While onions drop parades!

So peek beyond that curtain thin,
To worlds both round and square,
Where everything is sheer delight,
With giggles in the air!

Tides of Cosmic Possibility

In the tide of cosmic whims,
Where fish hold royal courts,
Kraken wear their crowns with pride,
As octopuses do retorts.

Stars play peek-a-boo from space,
While comets zoom and glide,
With cosmic jellybeans galore,
Each color, a surprise ride!

Planets spin their yarns all night,
With gravity that jigs,
And aliens throw confetti bombs,
While laughter surely brigs!

So ride the waves of what could be,
In seas of spark and glee,
Where every ripple sparks a laugh,
And possibility is free!

Abstractions of Otherworldly Journeys

In a realm where cats can fly,
And fish ride bikes, oh my oh my!
The birds wear hats, the clouds sing tunes,
While squirrels dance under the moons.

A toaster greets you with a cheer,
As waffles try to disappear.
Bananas chat with avocado friends,
In this world where time unbends.

A garden grows with jelly beans,
And rainbows spill from broken seams.
The trees wear shoes, the grass recites,
As laughter echoes through the nights.

So take a step through painted doors,
Where unicorns play card games on shores.
Each journey's filled with goofy fun,
In the realm of all that's never done.

Interstellar Chronicles

Far away in a galaxy wide,
Aliens ride on a comet's glide.
They sip on tea brewed from stardust,
And laugh at Earthlings' earthly rust.

Planets spin in a dizzy dance,
While robots take a silly chance.
With pogo sticks they bounce around,
In zero gravity, they astound.

Asteroids play tag, what a sight!
While meteors keep up the fight.
They all declare, 'We're here to stay!'
In the cosmic game of hide and play.

Spaceships painted like ice cream cones,
Zoom past planets made of stones.
In this corner of the vast unknown,
Laughter reigns, and fun has grown.

Dreams in Quicksilver

In dreams that shimmer like the sun,
Where jellyfish and rabbits run.
A world where socks can find their pairs,
And lollipops grow on pear tree flares.

Time slips and slides like a slippery eel,
Where every giggle is a big reveal.
Chickens put on beauty contests,
With judges that are fruit in plain vests.

In rivers made of chocolate streams,
Where children sail in bubble beams.
Ice cream mountains, oh what a treat,
Where candy corn is the common greet.

So ride your bike on a rainbow arc,
Through lands where laughter lights the dark.
In every corner, joy appears,
In a world that forgets its fears.

Poetic Divergences

In a land where clocks tick backward,
And every step leads to laughter heard.
Sunflowers wear tutus with sass,
As giraffes play hopscotch on grass.

Bottles talk and tell tall tales,
While whispering winds fill amusing sails.
The grass aims to tickle all your toes,
In a world where silliness grows.

Fish in top hats ride bicycles too,
While clouds form shapes of cartoon crews.
Each twist and turn is a delight,
In this bizarre, enchanting flight.

So swing from vines of bubblegum,
And join the dance of the hyperdrive drum.
Chart your course through this curious realm,
Where whimsy always takes the helm.

Enigmas in Existential Space

In a world where cows can fly,
Penguins wear tuxedos with style,
The sun is green and clouds are shy,
Llamas dance to works of Bach's smile.

Time ticks backward, that's the craze,
As clocks get dizzy, round they spin,
The walrus wears a purple maze,
While laughing cats give life a grin.

Fish hold meetings in the air,
To discuss who'll swim in tea,
A unicorn gets stuck in hair,
And puns float by, quite joyfully.

This cosmos laughs in all its schemes,
Where jellybeans are food for thought,
And everyone has tangled dreams,
Oh, what a mess that time has brought!

Reflections of Other Selves

In mirrors where the frogs all prance,
With hats and tails like fancy folks,
They teach the snails to do a dance,
While singing out their silliest jokes.

A wizard sneezes, sparks fly wide,
Creating worlds of candy lanes,
Where gumdrops thrived and dreams abide,
And lemon drops whisper their gains.

Here, my twin plays chess with a cat,
While pondering the meaning of life,
They giggle at the thoughts of that,
And debate the merits of strife.

So many selves in one small place,
All laughing at our mismatched shoes,
And every grin is a new embrace,
As we play hide and seek with views.

Echoes from Elsewhere

Oh, the echoes from lands unknown,
Where time is served with extra cheese,
And socks and shoes have softly grown,
Into a dance that stirs the breeze.

The trees wear glasses, read a book,
While crickets tap a jazzy tune,
The rivers glow, the oceans look,
For laughter's sake, beneath the moon.

Each sound a giggle, a happy tune,
Echoing through the fields of bliss,
With chubby squirrels who hope to swoon,
At the prospect of a nutty kiss.

So listen close, you might just find,
A distant chuckle, bright and clear,
In fun dimensions, laughter twined,
In every whisper, joy draws near.

Harmonies of the Untraveled

Out where the jellybeans all sing,
And rhythm rides on bubblegum,
You'll find a world with dancing bling,
Where silly songs and laughter come.

A space where hats can take a stroll,
And coffee beans recite their tales,
The polka dots play rock and roll,
As whimsy spins its playful sails.

With teapots swirling in delight,
And spoons who dream of flying high,
They harmonize 'til every night,
Is filled with sparks that light the sky.

From notes of dreams and giggles bright,
The music weaves its quirky lines,
A melody of sheer delight,
In worlds of laughter, how it shines!

www.ingramcontent.com/pod-product-compliance
Lightning Source LLC
Chambersburg PA
CBHW072214070526
44585CB00015B/1332